I0453178

"Silence" was published by the Jackpine Writers' Bloc in Talking Stick Volume 24 in 2015.

"Art on the Move" and "Warning' were published by the Jackpine Writers' Bloc in Talking Stick Volume 25 in 2016.

"Angel Choir" and "Missing Mom" were published by the Jackpine Writers' Bloc in Talking Stick Volume 28 in 2019.

"When Death Came" was published by the Jackpine Writers' Bloc in Talking Stick Volume 29 in 2020.

Very Much Alive: Pieces of My Mind on Paper

© 2026 by Jenn Jones Nienaber
ISBN number is 979-8-9942144-0-4

Published in the United States of America by paper&clouds

_____

Book cover graphic and interior design by: Jenn Jones Nienaber
Photography: © Mary Jones

VERY MUCH ALIVE

PIECES OF MY MIND ON PAPER

Poems

Mary Jensen Jones
with Jenn Jones Nienaber

Mom and Zoey, my Boston Terrier.

Missing Mom

When life has smashed your
head against the rocks and you
lie bruised and bleeding
face down in the dirt,
you long to hear her voice.
You crave her soothing words.

There, there, she'd say,
It's just a scratch – here let me kiss it.
He didn't mean it.
They were just teasing.
Winning's not the only thing.
The important thing is that you did your best.
There are other fish in the sea.
Tomorrow is another day.
You'll soon be good as new.
Go to sleep now.
Think happy thoughts.

Her dying tore
a ragged gaping hole in
the fabric of your life.
You could not mend it, could
not bind the raveled edges, even with
the tiniest stitches or the finest thread.

You're older now than
she was when she died.
You miss her every day.

© *Mary Jones, 2019*

Sitting on "Milt's bench" in Duluth, Minnesota.

INTRODUCTION

Compiling this book of Mom's poetry has been therapeutic. I hear her voice between the lines. I see her on the white couch in her living room, surrounded by the throw pillows I made her years ago. She has a beautiful journal in her hands. A good pen.

A small dog is perched behind her gazing out the window, or next to her pressed against her hip. It could be any one of the small dogs she babysat during the warmer months: Hero or Izzy. Or maybe the other Izzy.

Mom wrote in the morning, with a cup of coffee loaded with cream and sugar. But never too early, for she was a night owl and rarely saw the sunrise. By noon, she was ready to put the pen down, move around, think about running some errands or head out to her pool.

The words seemed to have come easily as she remembered her experiences. These poems cover a lifetime. Her lifetime.

Falling asleep on her favorite aunt's couch in Iowa.

Feeling, as a young mom, overwhelmed and outnumbered by the kids.

Stories of marriage and relationships; some of them hers, some not.

And as she approached 80, she relived moments and imagined new ones.

Occasionally, she would email a new poem to my sister Julie and me, which we largely ignored; not on purpose, but with small kids and big jobs it was hard to give them the attention they deserved.

I wish I had found the time.

Days later when I'd call her during my 30-minute commute home, the question would be posed:

"Did you get my email? The one with the poem?"

"Ah, yes, I saw it. I need to go back and read it."

"I know you're busy…"

I wish I had found the time. Instead of doom scrolling on my phone, I could have gone back to that email and given it the time and energy it deserved.

So, here I am. Reading and studying her words, wishing I could ask where the ideas, the words, the inspiration came from. How did each evolve? Were there iterations? How did she decide when they were complete, if they ever were?

...... I'm sorry, Mom. I should have made the time. I'm making it now.

Mom's death was not expected. She was living on her own until she made that 3am call asking me to bring her to the hospital. It was the middle of the summer, and she was living her best life: driving, shopping, swimming with her neighbors in their condo · pool. Until she wasn't.

She died August 7, 2021, surrounded by family and listening to Mozart. After three unsettling weeks in the ICU, starting in fear, moving into hope, and, finally, finishing in heartbreak, we said goodbye.. She was 78. I was 49.

Her mother, Grandma Alice, died in 1976, at the age of 68. Mom was 33. I was three. I didn't get to know Mom's mom. But I have faint memories and stories from Mom and older cousins. I know Mom missed her every day. I can't imagine the grief she felt when she had to share it with three small kids.

This book is in Mom's honor. This book is to share her words with the world. The words she wanted to share. Her words that deserve to be out there.

TABLE *of* CONTENTS

But this is a poem,
and the only characters here are you and I,
alone in an imaginary room
which will disappear after a few more lines

       – Billy Collins, excerpt from *The Great American Poem*

Grandpa Andy, Uncle Tim, Grandma Alice, Mom. 1945.

FAMILY

Family was important to Mom. She grew up in a family of four: father, mother, brother, sister. Their family was considered small for the 1940s; it was the aunts and uncles and cousins that made it large. Her father, Andy, had a younger brother, Neil, and baby sister, Ann. But Mom's mother had eleven siblings. And seven of them were sisters. And they were close.

I have a photo of the sisters all lined up in their nice dresses, likely in front of their parents' farmhouse. They are all smiling, a couple of heads are thrown back. There is a familiarity that can only be found amongst a gaggle of sisters.

It is these women, these aunts, that Mom remembers in the first poem, *Angel Choir*. I can picture each of them at the table, sipping from cups and saucers, the table speckled with crumbs of an apple cake or the remnants of lemon bars. I had been at that Iowa farm house when I was that same age, but I remember very little of it.

Mom grew up, met my dad, got married young, moved around, and then finally settled back in Minnesota with a young son. Four years later, they were surprised to find out she was expecting twins at a doctor appointment, introducing them to their girls: Julie and me. They had been hoping for just one.

She wrote about the three of us kids; our adventures and about the terror of loving her children. She wrote about her relationships with both my father and other family members. She wrote about her ultimate joy, her grandchildren. And she wrote about losing her own mother when they were both far too young.

Some of her writing was the truth. Some poems reveal family stories, while others are largely fictionalized. My father did not go fishing, at least not by choice. And much to my mother's disappointment, she never owned a convertible.

Grandma Alice with her brother Clarence and sisters Jennie, Clara, Mary and Emma, 1928.

Angel Choir

Someone must have forgotten to put me to bed
that night because I remember falling asleep
on the couch in Aunt Jennie's parlor,
dark red upholstery, white lace doilies,
clock ticking on the mantel,
fire's dying embers warming the room.

In the dining room, my aunts and my mother,
the only ones still up,
were talking late into the night.
"She's fallen asleep," one of them said.
"Leave her there – it's a shame to wake her."
I was still awake but didn't let them know.
I wanted to eavesdrop.

Their voices rose and fell
Now forte, now pianissimo
First one, then two, then all three at once
Aunt Mary's tenor, Aunt Jennie's soprano,
Mother's alto somewhere in between

Thoughtful pauses, playful teasing, bits of gossip
Aunt Mary's wisecracks,
Aunt Jennie's tinkling laughter,
Mother's gentle reminder not to wake me.

© Mary Jones, April 2015

Bad Day

On a late afternoon in mid-July,
The air conditioning rolled over and died
The kitchen was an inferno as the relentless sun
streamed through the windows
Like
Sweat poured down my face like
My twin babies fussed over God-knows-what
In their highchairs,
faces and hair smeared with mashed bananas
Little boys ran in and out of the house

slamming doors, yelling, asking for popsicles and Kool-Aid.
Sweat pouring down my face,
I screamed inwardly
    And wished myself somewhere else.

I would have run away except −
I was not wearing shoes and could not find my car keys.

© *Mary Jones, February 2003*

Love and Terror

The moment I had a baby was the moment I understood terror,
my heart blown sideways with adoration and fear. How dazzling
and how awful to love someone this much.

— Alison McGhee, from "Shall I Jump Now"

I once saw a sparrow
chase a hawk, saw it nip at the hawk's
heels like a sheepdog nipping at a sheep.
I knew at once the sparrow had to be a mom.

I've chased a few hawks in my life. I've
known the same love, the same terror…

… when my infant daughter
struggled to breathe and we rushed her
to the hospital.

… when years later my other daughter
didn't come home
one night and I was sick with worry,
imagining her mangled body dead
by the side of the road.

… when my son called to say
he'd crashed the car but he was fine,
just a little shaken up.

No one told me
how tenacious the love would be.

No one warned me about the terror.

© *Mary Jones, November 2015*

Make Believe

I'm the witch,
riding on my broom,
  cackling, "I'll get you my pretty!"
I'm the dragon,
breathing fire, roaring,
  my terrible tail trailing behind me.
I'm the monster
  clomping through the house,
    creating chaos as I go.
I'm the naughty student
  who doesn't listen, talks in class,
    forgets to raise her hand.

She's the little girl,
  squealing, giggling
    running away, hiding
    to escape the witch,
    the dragon, the monster.
She's the crabby teacher,
  threatening to call my mother
    if I don't behave.

The dog is the witch's pet frog
  or she is a unicorn, and
    sometimes she is just the dog.

I love that I get all the best parts.

© Mary Jones, March 3, 2015

Morning Thoughts

Six a.m. and suddenly I'm
wide awake, jolted out of a
dream by thunder. Too early to get up
so I lie there and listen
to the rain and think
about my mom. She would have loved this

early morning storm, would have leapt right
out of bed, gone to start the coffee, crack
the eggs into the pan. I can
still hear her chirping, "Rise and shine!"
She was always so
relentlessly cheerful, especially
in the morning, my least favorite
time of day.

Long before
the days of cell phones and
caller ID, when you never knew who was
on the other end, she would
answer the phone by saying
"Heaven" instead of "Hello".
What would
she answer now,
now that she's really there?

© *Mary Jones, April 2013*

A Rainy Day Tale

     It rained all afternoon
and the kids were restless.
They had played with every toy,
read every book,
watched every DVD.
Or so they said.

     Now they were turning
on one another, verbal jousts and not so
subtle kicks and slaps. Naked Barbie dolls
with hopelessly tangled blonde hair, Lego
blocks and tiny weapons of mass destruction
littered the family room floor. The dog was
licking peanut butter off the carpet while
the cat cowered under the couch.

     And their mother,
trying to get the laundry done, the bills paid,
and the house cleaned,
was running out of patience.
     And their father,
on a fishing trip, was not there to back her
up with a well-timed, "You heard your
mother!" (words that always
seemed to work)

So when the doorbell rang
and it was a politician, she lost it.
"I don't care which party you represent."
she screamed. "Take your tax breaks for
millionaires and your Obamacare and put
them where the sun don't shine. Buzz off,
buster!" (she used stronger language, but
this is a PG-rated poem)
And she slammed the door.

When she turned around, her
children stood before her open-mouthed,
aghast at hearing her use the words they
were not supposed to say EVER.

And for the
rest of the day they were subdued
and peaceful, allowing her to take a long
bubble bath, Mozart playing
on her iPod.

© *Mary Jones, October 2014*

Television Circa 1950

Father bought it for one hundred dollars,
a huge sum in those days.
He was so proud of his purchase
even though Mother complained
about the cost.

Still she watched with us
as we sat transfixed
by the black and white glow
of the tiny screen.
Four pairs of eyes in the
darkened living room
mesmerized by Milton Berle.

Suddenly we were famous,
the first family on the block to have TV.
Neighbor kids trooped home
with us after school to park themselves
in front of the TV, first the test pattern,
then Kukla, Fran and Ollie
at 4 o' clock.

Mother fretted about the dirt
the kids dragged in
and the noise they made
and the cookies they consumed.

Rules were imposed. No more
than two friends at a time, so
my brother and I
squabbled about whom to include.
All my friends annoyed him and I did not
like his either. Mother
said, if we were going to fight about it,
nobody could come over.

Then my brother declared that Kukla, Fran
and Ollie was for babies anyway and went
outside to ride his bike with his friends.

And when Susie rang the doorbell asking if I
could play, I turned the TV off and went outside.

The tiny screen went dark,
at least until after supper, and Mother
breathed a sigh of relief.

© *Mary Jones, November 2015*

The Wall

Brick by brick I built the wall
so that I couldn't see his pointing finger,
his scowling face, couldn't
hear his angry words.

Over the years the wall proved sturdy.
But I also didn't see him
hug my children or pet my dog,
didn't hear his laughter or his jokes,

Then in the sunny
dayroom of his nursing home,
when my dad knew he was dying,
the wall began to crumble
as we talked and I saw
the hurting little boy inside the
withered old man.

Snow fell the day he died.
covering up the last remaining bricks,
making everything new.

© *Mary Jones, 2016*

Warning

Right now,
they listen to you,
tell you they love you, bring you
bouquets of dandelions.

They tell you
what happened at school, what they
learned, who their friends are,
what they had for lunch.

They ask you
if you'll go with their class on a field trip,
if you'll take them to the zoo, the circus,
the playground.

Right now,
they need you to
take care of them – feed them,
clothe them, read to them,
guide them, answer their questions,
interpret the world.

And you have such
dreams for them – they'll be athletes,
musicians, rocket scientists.
They'll find a cure for cancer,
create dazzling works of art.

But someday soon,
without a backward glance,
they will shrug off the
burden of your expectations
as easily as they
would shed a jacket on a warm day.

They will laugh at your
warnings as they gallop off
into the future like frisky colts,
where they will learn things
you cannot teach them,
where they will go places
you cannot follow.
Just as you did years ago.

© *Mary Jones*

Seasons

"One season following another, laden with happiness and tears"
– from "Sunrise, Sunset"

Fiddler on the Roof

Take a day in early May
Add brilliant sunshine and lilac-scented air
Throw in apple trees raining pink petals on the ground
Add a convertible and put it on a country road
Make it candy-apple red
Put a young couple in the front seat
Color her beautiful; color him besotted
Make her gaze at him adoringly
Put a blue scarf in her blond hair
Put sunglasses and a huge smile on his face
Place a picnic basket in the back seat
and a golden retriever beside it
Let the wind part his fur and blow his ears inside out.

Fast forward twenty years
but make it December
Add sleet and snow
Swap out the convertible for a mini-van
Make it silver, no, make it beige
Put a middle aged couple in the front seat.
Color her resentful; color him stubborn
Make her turn away from him and look out the window,
arms crossed in front of her
Put a frown on his face
Put two sullen teenagers in the back seat
Have them argue with each other
Make the woman turn around and scold
while the man stares straight ahead.

Fast forward another twenty years
Make it July this time
Make the sun hot and the countryside lush and green
Substitute a convertible for the mini-van
Make it fire engine red, no, electric blue
Put an elderly couple in the front seat
Color him happy; color her content
Put a yellow scarf in her gray hair
Put a suntan and creases on his face
Make him smile at her
Put two lively children in the back seat
Make them chatter non-stop and ask
"Are we there yet?"
Make the woman turn around and answer them
Have the man laugh.

Fast forward again twenty years
Make it an October day
Color the leaves scarlet and gold and yellow
Make the car black
Have a motorcycle ride in front of it and
several other cars follow.
Color the woman inside grieving
Color the others sad
Have them wipe away tears and
speak in hushed tones.
Then have them smile as she talks
about all the other times she's been
down this road –
so many cars, so many seasons, so much
happiness, so many tears.

© *Mary Jones, May 2016*

Mom, while in high school, with her family dog.

DOGS

Gigi was Mom's first dog of her very own. I don't know when she got her, but I know early in marriage, she bred Gigi and helped deliver three little poodles. After my brother was born, Gigi went to live with Mom's parents.

We didn't get a family dog until I was seven or eight. Corky was a scruffy, black Cocker Spaniel who bore a hole straight into our hearts the moment we picked her up. Six months later, those hearts were shattered when we had to give her away. She shed too much. Mom's allergies were too severe.

A few years later, we started babysitting other people's dogs. All shapes and sizes, though never large. Sniffer (Beagle mix) and Chelsea (2.5 lb Yorkie) were regulars as their owner traveled frequently for work. There was Charlie and then another Charlie. And at some point we watched a friend's little fuzzy Bichon Frisé.

This little ball of white fur, who looked like a marshmallow with eyes, flipped a switch in Mom's head and the next thing I knew, we were picking up our own Bichon puppy.

The breeder said she was hypoallergenic. And Bijou proved she was both a non-allergen and the happiest, sweetest dog. I confessed to her all my middle school and high school traumas. She knew when you needed a kiss or just a cuddle. If there was a lap in the room, she was on it.

But dogs don't live long enough, and in my sophomore year of college, we had to say goodbye to Bijou. Mom, Julie and I all went to the vet, though we let Mom stay in the room with Bijou to say her final goodbye. Dad couldn't get away from work, or wasn't strong enough to say goodbye in person. Perhaps the latter.

Daisy was Mom's next Bichon. And because we were now out of the house, Daisy belonged to Mom and only Mom. She was stubborn and opinionated but was beyond loyal to Mom.

After Daisy, Mom started dogsitting again. She had a rolling list of clients who would stay with her anywhere from one night to a few weeks. Usually these little dogs slept in Mom's bed. One was deaf. Two were named Emmy. But Hero was her favorite. He was a small Cavalier King Charles Spaniel and reminded us all so much of Bijou. Attentive and generous with his love.

Her summer was booked with dogs. In the winter, when the ice and snow and sidewalks were unpredictable, she took a break. Except for Hero. And maybe Emmy.

The following pages reflect how much she cared for these little dogs. Her words show how much she loved them, and in turn, how much they loved her.

For Now

Outside huge flakes of silent
snow fall thickly to the frozen earth.

My little dog sprawls
across the back of the couch
like a rag doll thrown by a careless child.

She dreams of chasing squirrels
through fields of clover,
while I stretch out next to her,
watch her steady breathing.

I have everything I need,
a cup of fragrant tea
sonatas on the stereo,
a new book − and the time to read it.

I am soon lost within
its pages while Mozart wafts
across the room and fills my soul with peace

She sleeps; I read
We are content and life is good −
                    for now.

© Mary Jones, 2/11/03 latest revision 11/04/20

January Walk

Sun rises like an orange in the
eastern sky
Smoke billows from
chimneys. Giant icicles
hang from the eaves.

The dog does not want to go out
but it has to be done.
I put her coat on, then mine, then hat,
mittens, scarf and boots
and we venture forth into the
bone-chilling cold.

The arctic wind blows her ears
inside out, parts the fur on her face.
But she knows what to do
and she quickly creates
a patch of yellow in the snow
before we race back
to the comfort of the house.

© *Mary Jones*

Lost Dog

The sign is faded now
Wind and rain and sun
have torn its plastic cover off
and bleached the image.
Below the large block letters,
a picture of a smiling yellow lab
in happier days
before he was lost.
And then a phone number.
That's all.
Not the dog's name or where he
was last seen.

I've named him Sam in my imagination
I imagine he was last seen chasing
a rabbit, so distracted by his pursuit that
he didn't hear them calling him,
or chose to ignore them,
being young and
foolhardy and disobedient.

He chased the rabbit
through backyards and fields and maybe
all the way to the river. Then he
discovered he was lost. Muddy and cold,
burrs clinging to his fur, I imagine he
ended up on the doorstep
of an elderly couple that I'll call
George and Martha, who took him in,
cleaned him up, fed him, gave him water,
called the phone number on his tag.

I imagine Sam is back home now
where he lifts his great golden head
to smile at his people
and run around in crazy circles
at the dog park
and come home to warm himself
before a blazing fire.

Period. End of story.

Any other outcome is unthinkable.

© *Mary Jones, November 2016*

Some Questions about Dogs

Even though there are a dozen balls
in the backyard,
why is it that the only ball the dog wants
is the one that bounced too high
on the patio
and went over the fence?

Why is it that the dog always
waits until you are on the phone
to start barking at
nothing in particular?

How can a ten-pound dog take
up half of a queen-size bed?

Why is it they hate walking in the rain
but love walking in mud and
tracking it everywhere?

How do they know it's you
before you even walk in the door?

Why is it that the one person at your
party who doesn't like dogs
is the person whose lap
they jump into?

Why do they cock their heads to one side
when you're talking to them?

Why do they always leave us before we're
ready for it?

Why is their love so long?
Why are their lives so short?

© *Mary Jones, June 2016*

Stray Dog

He's out there again. She knows.
She's seen him from
her lookout post on the couch.
She races around from
window to window
sounding the alarm.
Then he trots into other yards.
And the dogs outside
sound the same alarm.
She begs to be let out but
I don't do it. Soon he leaves the street,
the barking outside dies down.
But still she growls, more quietly,
and will not be calmed down
until her dinner dish is filled.

© *Mary Jones, 5/11/03*

The Ballad of the Patient Dog

She sits beside the bathroom door
imploring me with her eyes.
I've seen that hangdog look before –
she needs her exercise.

But sweetie, I say, you'll have to wait,
I need to dry my hair.
Until that's done, there's no debate.
We can't go anywhere.

She pays no mind to what I say,
but turns her whine up higher
and at the bathroom door she stays
'til I turn off the dryer.

We're all set now to go,
I tell her when I'm done.
But wait, there's something more to do
before we can be gone.

So I put on my socks and shoes
and start to fix my face.
I can tell she's not amused
as she chews on my shoelace

What are you waiting for, says she,
I thought we were going for a walk.
I need to sniff and poop and pee.
We need only go round the block.

We're down the stairs and almost ready.
I pause to put on my coat
and fasten her leash but she won't hold steady.
She's prancing like a frisky colt.
Then finally we're out the door
and her tail just won't stop wagging.
Her patience has found its reward,
not to mention her incessant nagging.

© *Mary Jones, April 8, 2017*

Winter Evening

I take the puppy out to do her business
in the newly fallen snow.
Head down, nose to the ground,
she moves through it
like a canine snowplow.
She runs in circles,
falls down, gets up,
rolls around.

Tired and cold, I bark at her to hurry up.
She looks at me and smiles
through a muzzle full of snow,
then barks back
"Hey, lighten up. This is fun!"
So I make snowballs for her to chase,
which she returns for me to throw again.
We both laugh and I'm no longer
cold and tired.

© Mary Jones

Mom and Dad on their wedding day, 1961.

RELATIONSHIPS

My parents were young when they got married. She was 18 and had just finished her first year of college. He was 22 and had just graduated. There was a job waiting for him in Milwaukee, managing a new Kroger store. But in 1961, she could not make such a move with him unless they were married.

In their wedding album she is beaming. Young, slim, wide smile. He is tall and handsome and still has hair.

They were married for nearly 52 years, until Dad passed from Lewy Body Dementia in 2013. His passing was expected and a relief, but the dementia took Dad away from us years earlier. His personality changed from patient and kind, to frustrated and angry. He asked to be moved to assisted living, then resented us when he did.

These poems touch on his struggle, but they also explore the controversies inherent in the institution of marriage. Marriage is not easy. But nobody ever said it was.

When I read these poems, I wonder how much of it is memory and how much of it is fiction. The canning, the fishing, the Pabst Blue Ribbon is all made up. But the rest of it? I don't know.

My husband and I dated for eight years before we got engaged and then married the following year. I won't call it pressure, but she certainly was not subtle when dropping hints about marriage and kids. When our daughter, Sky, was born, we spent more time together. We would meet for lunch or head to her pool. Every December, we would attend the Nutcracker Ballet. Mom became our go-to sitter when other plans fell through. Mom and Sky created a bond that revolved around play and laughter. Mom even taught Sky how to roll her eyes at a young age.

My parents raised three kids in a comfortable suburban home surrounded by friends and family. They valued education and kept us active with sports, a speed boat, and yearly vacations to wherever Dad's company sent him.

Nobody is perfect. No marriage is perfect.

Seeing that and acknowledging that is a gift.

Cold War

I

They stand posing for the camera behind
a three-tiered cake with a big gold 50 on top.
She looks grim despite her new floral dress,
pink corsage pinned above her ample bosom,
freshly permed mouse-brown hair.
He looks uneasy in a gray suit,
pink boutonniere in his lapel.
She frowns but he has plastered on a grin,
not wanting to disappoint the picture takers.

She would rather be in her kitchen canning
the rest of the summer's tomatoes.
He would rather be watching the Twins on TV
and nursing a Pabst Blue Ribbon.
They didn't want a party; on that much they agreed.

She doesn't know what the fuss is about –
fifty years of marriage only means you're old
and unwilling to divorce. It doesn't mean the
fifty years were happy.
He doesn't know what to think, hasn't had an
independent thought in years.

II

He wonders when the war started. Was it when
he didn't grieve sufficiently over their stillborn
first child? Or was it when he didn't crack the
whip the night their teenage son came home drunk?
Perhaps it was because he was content to remain in the
same job year after year, while her friends' husbands
moved up in the world.

She wonders when he stopped loving her. Was it when she criticized his mother? Or was it when she started gaining weight after their third child was born? Perhaps it was when he fell in love with that floozy at the office three decades ago. She never confronted him, but she saw the furtive looks that passed between them at the office Christmas party.

He resents the fact that she always got the best of him, always won every argument. He wishes he'd fought back a little more. She resents the fact that she always had to discipline the kids, talk back to tradesmen and store clerks, because he wouldn't.

III

They both know the marriage is a bleak landscape littered with the rubble of their unfulfilled dreams. Their kids know but pretend that all is well. Their friends and relatives and neighbors suspect it might be unhappy but are easily fooled because there have been no huge battles. No public criticism, only vague comments from time to time.
"Women, can't live with 'em, can't live without 'em,"
he would joke.
"You know how men are." she would sigh.

Their marriage has been like that stone in your shoe
you don't remove and soon you're limping a little
but after a while you get used to the pain
and people don't really notice because they have stones in
their own shoes to worry about.

IV

I could have done worse, he thinks. I might
have married Linda who ran off with her tennis coach.
Or Martha who ended up killing her husband
with a kitchen knife in a fit of rage.

I could have done worse, she thinks. I could have
married Stanley, who walked out on his wife and sons
forty years ago and has not been heard from since.
Or Roger who couldn't hold a job and
drank away his wife's paychecks.

Still, he thinks, she looks nice today. He never minded that
she put on weight although he knows she did.
She's always been a good cook
and she always laughed at his old tired jokes.

Still, she thinks, he has always been so easy-going,
so patient with the kids when they were growing up and
so playful with the grandkids now.

So today they'll smile and be polite and say
all the right things. They'll
go home, she to her canning,
he to his beer and baseball game,
and they'll go on, the way they always have.
The war will go on until one of them dies
and the survivor will finally
declare a truce.

© *Mary Jones, 12/17/14*

Poet's Dilemma

The words swim by like tropical fish in a tank,
yellow-striped, cobalt blue, orange with polka dots.
They float by like soap bubbles in the air,
their surfaces iridescent, multi-hued.
They bounce along the floor like balls in a pinball game,
careening off the couch, the table, the lamp.

Active verbs like "zoom" and "crash"
Abstract nouns like "mystery" and "epiphany"
Lovely adjectives like "luscious" and "silent"
Similes and metaphors without peer, original and stunning

You want to put your hand in the fish tank,
chase the bubbles, grab the balls and
stick them on the page where they belong.
You need them to populate your ideas. Your ideas

are vague and ephemeral without the words.
The harder you reach for them, the more
they retreat. Soon they're out the door,
flying up in the air like helium balloons,
or swimming into the gutters or
smashing into passing cars. Sometimes

they return – in dreams or in the shower,
usually when you can't write them down.
Sometimes they are gone forever, lost in
limbo where another poet could snatch them
and write your dazzling poems –
your worst nightmare.

© Mary Jones, March 9, 2015

The Dying of the Light

"Do not go gentle into that good night
Rage, rage against the dying of the light"

– Dylan Thomas

       It wouldn't be so hard
if he weren't so angry, if he didn't always beg
to go home. If he didn't babble such nonsense.
If he could converse again.

       Gone is the man she loved,
locked in dementia's dungeon, his
personality scrubbed clean of all the traits
that made him lovable –
humor, imagination,
thought itself.

       It wouldn't be so hard
if his expression weren't so blank,
his eyes so dead.

       Still she goes to see him, bringing
cookies, French fries, hamburgers, trying to
engage in conversation, telling him
of a new grandchild, telling him
that Harry died and that his hockey team
is having a good season.

       Sometimes love is hard.
It hurts to see the bright flame
of his lively wit
and sweet spirit be snuffed out.
It hurts to see his rage, his blank eyes,
and so she wonders
if her love for him is fading too.

Maybe love is not a feeling;
maybe love is a decision –
a decision to keep coming,
to make sure he's taken care of.

And she can do this,
even as she falls apart inside,
even when it's hard to watch
the dying of the light.

© Mary Jones, January 2015

Modern Day Poets

Poets used to write with
quill pens on parchment. They sat at ornate
gold–leafed desks, looked out of leaded windows on
ancestral estates, trying to describe the song of the skylark,
the colors of a sunset. There was a lot of iambic
pentameter involved.

They were
almost always male and wore shirts with open necks
and voluminous sleeves that got stained with ink
to the servants' dismay. They strolled
for hours in solitary woods, thinking of ways
to fit their words into elaborate rhyme schemes.

They didn't
need to earn a living, didn't need to milk the cows
or plow the fields or bake the bread.

Nowadays the poets all
have day jobs. We write in the tiny margins of
busy days. An hour stolen before the family
wakes up. A late night rendezvous in the den with
a notebook and a ballpoint pen.

When we say we
write poems, we are met with bewilderment. People
say it's nice, but what they really think is that it's weird.
A few of us get published; the rest
read their poems in coffeehouses.

But still we write because
the reward is in the doing, not the applause. We write
because we can't not write.

And so, my fellow poets,
I salute you. Let's drink a toast to all who
scribble in the shadows of Shakespeare. But don't
quit your day jobs.

If

If I had known you way back then,
Would you have liked me?
Would we have been friends?
Would you have been impressed by my jump rope skills
and my spelling bee championship?
Would I have been envious of your dancing lessons
and your nice house?
Would you have minded that I loved to sing
and you couldn't carry a tune?
Would I have cared that you had brand new clothes
and I wore hand-me-downs?

If I had gone to your house, would I
have noticed your mom's bruises and
the booze on your dad's breath?
Would I have told my mom?
If you had come to my house, would you
have noticed the threadbare carpet and
the empty fridge?
Would you have told your mom?
Would you have shared your sandwich when I
had none? Would I have let you sleep at my house
when you were afraid to go home?

I like to think so. I like to think
we would have sat at lunch, giggling
until milk came out of our nostrils,
whispering behind our hands
about the cool girls who
were too stuck-up to notice us.

I like to think we might have
saved each other.

© *Mary Jones, 1/15/12*

The Rocky Mountains, taken during a visit with Julie.

NATURE

Mom had a dish towel, which is now mine, that reads "I enjoy nature, sometimes I drink wine on a patio," which pretty much sums up how much time she spent out in the woods. On the other hand, if the summer sun was out, she was soaking it in.

When she was young, her family would venture to Lake Minnetonka to fish. She'd go with them, but I can't picture her with a fishing pole in her hands. Instead, she likely brought a book and sat on the edge of a rock and read through the long afternoon as her father, mother and brother watched their lines bob in the water.

Though she wasn't outdoorsy, the following poems prove that she was inspired and often saved by the natural world. Crows, considered one of the smartest birds, appear often in the following pages. As do songbirds and squirrels and even a tiny turtle who just wants to swim.

As I've gotten older, I have started noticing birds. Recognizing their different cries and songs. Marveling when I see a Pileated Woodpecker or hear the flapping of a hummingbird.

I am amazed by the way Mom can describe a scene or memory so fully, touching on all of our senses.

She alludes to rough days, which we all have, and how nature can turn a mood back around. It reminds me to slow down, get outside more often, hunt for acorns or perfect oak leaves, or even just have a chat with the little yellow finch perched in the tree outside my door.

I will let the squirrels continue to attack our bird feeders, will let the baby bunnies munch on my newly planted hostas, and will stop and watch as mama deer and her fawn cross the path.

These animals were here first, we are merely borrowing, or rather, encroaching on their space. At least I'd like to think that. Mom did too.

Rebuilding

A sudden storm snatched the wreath
off the front of my house,
sent it sailing to parts unknown.
It was a fake, made of silk
forsythia flowers,
but the house finches loved it.

For two summers, it had provided
a safe space for their nests
away from all predators except
the wild wind,
and now it was gone.
I grieved for the eggs that
would never hatch. I hoped Mama and Papa
had survived.

So I put up another wreath, made sure it
was fastened securely to the brick wall
Mama and Papa Finch scolded me from a nearby tree
thinking me the predator
who had swept away their nest. I was glad to
hear their loud rebuke. At least they were okay.

Later as I passed by the wreath,
something fluttered out from it,
flew to the tree and started scolding.
You've built a new nest, Mama Finch, I said.
Not a good location, I said
Are you sure you want it there? I asked

At that she broke out in joyous song
and I smiled.
Good luck to you,
may the winds be light
until the babies have fledged.

© *Mary Jones, September 2017*

Chickadees

Midnight in January
I lie awake
in my warm house
and wonder how the birds
survive this bitter cold.

Outside my bedroom wall,
deep within the branches
of a blue spruce,
a dozen chickadees
huddle closely together,
feathers fluffed up
to keep each other warm.

Tomorrow
in the bright arctic sunshine,
they will be at the feeder.
I will watch them
and marvel.

© *Mary Jones*

February

The White Witch has come,
has lured us into her sleigh,
promising candy.
Now we are forced to endure
one hundred years of winter

Outside her castle
endless snowstorms are raging
If we dare go out,
we fall on ice, get stuck in
snowdrifts, suffer frostbite.

Who can save us now?
Who can end this evil curse?
It's Aslan we need.
Only he can break the spell
And bring us blessed springtime.

© *Mary Jones, February 2019*

Judgment

The sun is hot
It burns my eyes
and stares into my soul.
Along the rocky shore
gulls scream and circle
and swoop down to tear at the flesh
of an unlucky fish
dropped by a careless pelican
I walk alone
and ponder what I did
to earn such judgment.
I walk alone
and wonder why it all went wrong –
why my swimming soaring life
crashed on the rocks

I hadn't asked for this
but neither had the fish.

© Mary Jones

June Morning – 5am

The crows started it,
squawking from one treetop to the next.
Other crows continued the alarms.
I wondered, as I lay there in bed, what
they were shouting. Were they telling one another
about choice morsels found on the road
or warning of predators?
Were they saying, "Here I am, where are you?"

The songbirds started in then,
robins and finches, cardinals and warblers
guarding their nests, proclaiming their territory,
singing with the joy of being alive,
having survived the perilous journey north
to their nesting grounds.
Or were they saying "Here I am, where are you?"

I thought of closing the window
but then I caught a whiff of the lilac tree outside.
I lay there listening and breathing in the fragrance,
and soon fell back to sleep
to lilac-scented dreams filled with birdsong, which
gave way to dreams of friends and family that I miss,
I woke up thinking, "Here I am, where are you?"

© Mary Jones, July 6, 2020

The Trouble with Peonies

The trouble with peonies is that they bloom in June
when sudden storms can smash them flat and leave
their brilliant blossoms, red and pink and white, strewn
all over lawns and fields. And gardeners who grieve

their passing then enclose the plants in cages
hoping that they will stay sturdy and upright
when next the inevitable wild tempest rages.
Sometimes this works and they find, to their delight,

blossoms unbowed by relentless rain and gale.
Sometimes the flowers still end up on the ground
in spite of all they do. Sometimes it hails
and gardeners find the petals beaten down.

I think I'd rather grow daisies and asters which flower
in August when calm winds make prospects less dour.

© *Mary Jones, March 2017*

Dragonfly

I am about to turn the page
But then he lands on my book.
Brilliant blue against the white
Fragile iridescent wings etched with tiny lines
Sequins in the sunlight
Enormous complex eyes
Black stripes (who knew?)
He pauses, seems to wonder
If the words on the page were edible
It was a book of poetry – ample nourishment
For my soul – but not for him.

© *Mary Jones*

Rescues

A tiny turtle
perched on the edge of the pool
"Please don't jump', we cried.
Our entreaties he ignored,
took the plunge. We saved him though.

A fledgling fallen
Helpless, squawking, on the ground
She was on horseback
Dismounting, she picked him up
Went home, called the DNR

Lifeless on the road
Victim of a hit and run
Poor furry gray squirrel
He attempted CPR
It worked. The squirrel ran away.

© *Mary Jones, 10/17/18*

Tiny Miracles

Maybe it was the way the sky looked –
          bright blue with thin high clouds, feathery edges
swirled around as if in some cosmic mixer,
and the plane, a shiny silver cylinder, hung
                    in mid-air on giant puppet strings,
Maybe it was the way the sunflowers,
                    impossibly gold,
swayed in the gentle breeze,
Maybe it was the way the cicadas
                    buzzed and droned in the sultry August air,
It could have been the way the peach,
          soft and sweet and tart, dribbled juices down my chin.
It could have been the crows' bright clamor in the treetops.
It could have been Bach on the radio.

This flood of tiny miracles
washed away the stones of sadness
from my soul
if only for a little while
on this ordinary summer day.

© *Mary Jones, 8/31/10*

Risk Assessment

Risk Assessment
He scoots down the trunk of an oak tree,
jaws clamped tight around an acorn,
             when suddenly he spots me,
waggles his head up and down,
             back and forth.

He pauses to consider
(if squirrels can be said to consider)
             whether to head back to
the safety of the treetop or
             whether he has time
             to get his treasure stored away
                    before he is attacked.

                    Still as a stone I stand
and watch. Tail twitching wildly,
he makes up his mind.
             He is going to risk it.

He scampers down the trunk,
scurries into the bushes.
             Safe, he thinks.

             I take a deep breath and walk on,
sorry for the drama I've created,
             yet happy for a chance to observe
this moment, one that must be
             repeated over and over
                    each day.

             For now he's safe.
Next time he may not be so lucky.

© *Mary Jones, September 2014*

Crows

Bullies of the avian playground,
knocking down smaller birds
just because they can.
Gangsters in the ghetto,
full of bluster and bravado,
swaggering around in black hoodies
and dark glasses.

They croak instead of sing.
They eat roadkill and the eggs of songbirds.
They pick through dumpsters and trash cans.

No wonder they get a bad rap.
No wonder people say they hate them.

Did you know they mate for life and mourn their dead?
Did you know they've learned to use simple tools?

As for me, I celebrate their boldness,
their dark-cloaked beauty,
their majestic throaty cries.

When summer's birds have flown
and taken with them their colorful
plumage and melodious songs,
I see crows sitting among
bare black branches against a gray sky
shouting to each other, their bright
clamor punctuating the silence,
and I can't help but smile.

© *Mary Jones, February 2016*

Lament

I hate the wind, the rain, the cold
I hate the early dark
I hate that golden hours have now turned brown.
Still I walk through
the dreary days of dark November.

The leaves at my feet, once gold and scarlet,
are pallid corpses now, discarded
like yesterday's newspaper.
Crows squabble over small limp bodies
on the pavement and geese
honk overhead on their journey south.

Children desert the playground to hunker down
inside in front of TV sets. Empty swings squeak eerily
in the wind as though inhabited by ghosts.
Abandoned barbecue grills,
where steaks sizzled all summer long, languish
on patios now that cooks have moved indoors.

Looming above me, the bare branches of an oak
point sinister fingers against leaden sky. Then
snow starts to fall, at first a
few tentative flakes, then snow so thick
I can hardly see the way ahead,
snowflakes landing on my face, my hands, my clothing,
covering the dead leaves. Perfect sparkling hexagons,
blessing all they touch.

© Mary Jones, March 3, 2015

On Seeing a Deer in the Front Yard

I saw her for an instant, sleek
and golden
in the light of the street lamp
But then the dog barked and she
bolted down the hill
into the woods
where she belongs.
I wondered why she'd come
because it was November and
the lilies she
feasted on all summer
in the garden out back
were dry and withered now
and the grass was dead.

Could it be she was just curious
about the people living here?
In the same way we invade her woods
was she now invading our space
to get a closer look at us?

Or maybe she was sent from God
who knew I'd had a horrid day
and needed something beautiful
to rest my eyes on,
if only for an instant.

© *Mary Jones, 1/23/04*
Revised 3/20/13

December

I can take the cold.
I don't even mind the snow.
The darkness I hate.
Late sunrise, early sunset,
in between gloomy gray skies.

So, I decorate.
I bake cookies and wrap gifts,
string lights on the tree,
go to concerts and parties
to make the season brighter.

And I take solace
in the midst of this dark time.
For with the solstice,
clearer brighter days will come,
each one longer than the last.

© *Mary Jones, January 2019*

Kamala Harris and Ruth Bader Ginsberg action figures.

POLITICS

I don't remember Mom sharing her political views when I was young. I know Dad was a proud Republican, but a Republican from the '80s, not the right-leaning MAGA Republicans of today.

But as I got older, and she got older, she voiced her political views loud and clear. She was inclusive and truly lived by The Golden Rule. Her liberal Presbyterian church was her lifeline and she served on the social action committee among others.

Injustices throughout the world tore through her soul and she writes about them in these poems. The pandemic was tough on her, as she lived alone. But she made the best of it with Zoom calls and long walks with neighbors and masks.

Life still wasn't back to normal when she entered the hospital in 2021. We still wore masks, I was still working from home, school was about to be back to normal a few weeks later.

I look at everything that has happened in the world since 2021 and sometimes I am grateful she hasn't had to deal with it.

Ukraine. Gaza. Our Administration. ICE. The Supreme Court. Target. Stripping DEI...

So many times in the last four years I have said to myself, "At least Mom isn't here to see this."

It's a thin and fractured silver lining.

I'm glad she had the strength to stand up for others, because as Mr. Rogers said, Look for the helpers."

Mom was a helper.

Art on the Move

I'm already running late when
I have to stop for a freight train.
I'm in no mood to be entertained,
yet the graffiti rushing by on
the plain brown boxcars
dazzles me.

Oddly shaped letters and designs,
pulsing with energy,
brilliant blues, vibrant pinks, neon greens,
always outlined in black,
simple messages,
some profane, some silly.

I picture the artists, under cover of
night, sneaking around railroad yards
in some distant city
carrying spray cans of paint.
Maybe they wear ski-masks and carry
flashlights. Maybe one of them
keeps a look-out for police.

I suppose this is a crime, but I would
not arrest them. I might even hold
the flashlight.

© *Mary Jones*

I Remember

I remember wearing a brown tweed coat
a sweater, pleated skirt,
penny loafers with brown knee socks
that blustery sleety November day
that JFK was murdered.
I remember seeing Jackie on the news,
her bright pink suit stained with blood.
I remember hearing the Navy hymn,
"Eternal Father Strong to Save," on the radio
as I woke up the next day.
I remember weeping for my country
because a beloved president was dead.
I remember the flags being at
half-staff for a month.

I remember wearing a blue linen dress
and white pumps that sunny September day
the towers came down.
I remember seeing people on TV
running down the street, hands over their mouths,
while clouds of ash rained down over their heads.
People jumping out of the towers to certain deaths.
I remember hearing Samuel Barber's
"Adagio for Strings" as I drove home from work.
Again the flags were lowered.
Three thousand perished.
I remember weeping for my country.

I don't remember what I was wearing
on the day the plague came and the world closed down.
I remember the clouds of uncertainty and fear
raining down on our heads for months on end.
I remember seeing pictures of makeshift morgues,
mass graves and exhausted health care workers.

I remember conflicting accounts from politicians and doctors.
I remember wearing a teal blouse and beige pants
and bare feet that warm September day when the numbers
of US dead reached two hundred thousand.
I remember weeping for my country.
No flags were lowered, no music played.

I remember our president saying, "It is what it is."

© *Mary Jones, 9.27.20*

Lockdown Lament

At first I was fine
I had lots of books to read
I got rid of things
I don't use and didn't need
Organized at breakneck speed

Then I went shopping
Getting groceries is a chore
Now I wear a mask
Empty shelves throughout the store
It's just not fun anymore

No movies, no plays,
No concerts to attend now
I don't see my friends.
Since haircuts are not allowed,
my hair hangs past my eyebrows

I haven't lost much
I'm only inconvenienced
So many have died
Lost jobs are a just grievance
Suffering that makes no sense

No this is not fun
This may last quite a long time
When will it be done?
Will a victory be won?
We're all in this together

© Mary Jones, May 5, 2020
Revised May 9, 2020

Storms

Summer skies turn ominous
Thunder rumbles, lightning flashes
Rain falls in sheets
Beaches empty out and people race to cars
Picnickers take shelter
Children abandon backyards to go inside
Radar weather maps turn yellow and red
as weather men track the storm

Afterwards people assess the damage
Limbs of trees across roads
Flooding in low areas
Power outages
People stand in the rubble of their homes
and tell reporters they are lucky to be alive
Homes can be rebuilt, they say,
but a life lost is forever
Everyone goes about their lives.

Wintry skies turn leaden
Icy winds blow horizontal snow
Traffic slows to a crawl
Cars spin out on freeways
Multiple crashes ensue
Schools and businesses close
People stay indoors and wait it out
Roofs collapse under the weight of
Five inches, six, a foot or more of snow

Afterwards people shovel out
Roads are plowed
New roofs are erected
Tree limbs felled by ice are removed
Cars are repaired
Schools open and people go back to work
Everyone goes about their lives

Gunshots, followed by screams and sobs
In theaters, in nightclubs, on city streets
Gunshots by police against civilians
or by snipers against police
Planes fly into skyscrapers
A truck weaves into a crowd of people
watching fireworks at a beach.

Bombs go off in crowds watching a marathon
Bombs go off at airports and in shopping malls
New York, Paris, Brussels, Orlando, Istanbul,
Saint Paul, Baton Rouge, Dallas, Munich ...
The list goes on and on

Afterwards, people mourn the dead
and take the injured to hospitals
They clear away the rubble,
begin rebuilding
Prayers are offered up for victims and survivors

Everyone is long on blame, short on solutions
People call for gun control
They vow to fight terrorism
They march to protest police brutality
People call for increased police presence
People call for stricter laws
People urge compassion and restraint

Then the furor dies down
People seem to forget until the next storm
comes hard on the heels of the last one.
Another and another and another...

Everyone goes on about their lives.
Or do they?

© *Mary Jones*

Annual Halloween party with the Red Hats, 2015.

GROWING OLD

This may be the hardest section to read, but maybe also the closest to knowing Mom. Dad passed away in 2013 after a year in a care facility. He had struggled with Lewy Body dementia for years before that, though we don't know exactly when it came on.

These poems are honest and reflect the loneliness she felt at this stage of her life.

She writes here about missing Dad and missing us kids and how she filled that space with music and words.

She writes about how she wants to be remembered and how she wanted to celebrate the end of her life. I'm only sorry I didn't find those words until after her celebration of life. How fun would it have been to have a parade and trumpets?

She writes about finally accepting herself, her flaws, her features, her strengths. I hope she knows that she was loved, and considered brilliant in the eyes of many.

Her friends tell me how she would always light up the room, how so many considered her to be their best friend, how they would miss her wit and laughter.

There is no rewind, like she writes. But there is recall and memories and her words. She didn't get to 80, which makes me sad. She should have. She was taken too soon. Before she had a chance to do a final bloom.

But I know she was tired. Tired of the pain in her knees and her back and her jaw. The fibromyalgia which she struggled with for years had taken so much away from her. But she was also tired emotionally, from the crazy politics of this world, the wars and violence and policies that wore her down so severely.

At the end, while she was in the hospital, unable to move, not able to speak, I like to think she was ready to say goodbye. It wasn't cancer or a car accident or a hot air balloon crash that ended her life. Instead, it was a tiny, red iron pill that found its way into her lung and slowly tore a hole in the right lobe.

By the time she knew it was there, she had lost too much blood and went into cardiac arrest. Two weeks later, after a rollercoaster of hope and dispair, we learned she had suffered a stroke in her brain stem.

She would never again be able to eat or read or write. It was not the ending she would have written. Clearly, she was not in her *French Villa* or her *New York apartment* or sitting on *The Beach* like she imagined on the page. But I hope in those last days she travelled there in her mind. Returned to the places she loved while she was getting ready to return to the people she loved.

As we talked to her in those final moments, we told her to look for Dad, for Aunt Ann, for the dogs who never lived long enough and had gone before her. And to look for her mother, who she missed every single day. Just like I miss her. Every day.

On Turning Eighty

After "On Turning Ten" by Billy Collins

The whole idea of it makes me feel
like my life is surging forward with something,
Something far better than any praise
or awards or prizes I won in my early years,
a kind of booster shot of confidence,
a feeling of being comfortable in my own skin,
a transforming of my very soul.

You tell me it is too late to be looking forward
but that is because you have no idea
how stressed I felt at twenty,
trying to navigate my college years,
and how besieged I felt at thirty, a mother with
three young children and no time to call her own,
and how empty I felt at fifty when they all left home.
And how sad I was at seventy when my husband died.

So now I am mostly at the window
watching the early afternoon light.
Back then it never fell so joyfully
on the delicate spring foliage in my yard.
And my car never gleamed in my driveway
as it does today,
all its brilliant redness waiting to go on adventures.

This is the beginning of wholeness, I say to myself,
as I shuffle through the universe in my orthopedic shoes
It is time to say goodbye to old dreams and illusions,
time to turn the next big number

It seems only yesterday I used to believe
that life had broken me and I was too injured to go on.
If you cut me, I would bleed out.
But now that I've been through all life could throw at me,
I know I will survive.

© *Mary Jones, April 2019*

Dreams

I'm singing in the choir, all the wrong notes because
I've lost my place. My choir robe is missing,
in its place my witch costume from the second grade.

Then I'm taking a final in a college classroom.
I don't remember ever having gone to class or
what the subject is. All I know is that I'm unprepared.

Then I'm driving in a car with my children, all of them
small again, in a relentless rainstorm. I can't see
the road ahead and they're all crying.
Suddenly my mom appears, calms
them down, turns on my windshield wipers.
I turn to thank her but she's gone.

Next thing I know I'm inside a murder mystery.
Friends from various times
of my life are fellow sleuths or victims and perps.
There are spies and government secrets.
The bad guy seems to be my
sweet old grandpa, which I refuse to believe.

The scene shifts – now I'm running late for work,
first day of a new job. I try to call but can't get through.
When I do they don't speak English, can't
understand me. I'm sure I'll be fired.

Then suddenly I am back in the choir,
My witch costume gone, but now I'm naked
in front of the congregation. We start to
sing and the most sublime Mozart issues forth from our lips.
It's my radio and I'm awake again.

What a relief! I haven't lost my place in choir or my robe,
my kids are grown up and safe, my grandpa isn't guilty,
I graduated from college decades ago and I never lost that job
or any other just for being late.

All those adventures have made me
hungry. So I make coffee
and oatmeal with brown sugar and raisins,
grateful for reality.

© Mary Jones, 11/18/13

Final Wishes

When I die, don't you dare cry for me.
Sing no sad songs, breathe no deep sighs.
Go to the zoo, fly a kite, plant a tree,
don't just sit there in the dark and cry.

Instead of a funeral, you must have a celebration
full of flowers, full of singing, full of laughter.
I simply won't permit any speculation
about my soul and where I'll spend hereafter.

There should be lots to drink and lots to eat
and a big band and dancing to bid me farewell.
A parade with trumpets would also be sweet,
playing Dixieland and Sousa marches as well.

Of course if you can't do this, I'll understand.
I won't be attending so it's out of my hands.

© *Mary Jones, June 2014*

Good Enough

When she was young and pretty,
she stared into the mirror
a dozen times a day
looking for imperfections.
She found them everywhere.

Her chin was too pointed.
her midriff too bulgy,
her chest too flat,
her eyes had bags under them,
and here and there a tiny pimple
had erupted on her forehead.

Glamour and Seventeen
showed her how to make herself
more attractive –
use the right eyeshadow,
the right concealer, the right lipstick,
wear the right clothes to conceal her figure flaws,
stand up straight, walk gracefully, be confident.
And on and on, ad nauseum.

No one told her
she was good enough as is.
She didn't know she had a lovely smile
even without lipstick.
She didn't know her eyes were bright
even without eyeshadow.

Then one day, fifty years later
she looked into the mirror
at her face full of wrinkles,
her body grown more ample,
her hair now turned gray, her pointed chin,
her too flat chest, her baggy eyes,
and she pronounced herself
Good. Enough.

© *Mary Jones, August 2016*

Home Movies

But you can't jump the track, we're like cars on a cable,
and life's like an hourglass glued to the table.
No one can find the rewind button, girl,
so cradle your head in your hands and breathe, just breathe.

                                 – *"Breathe" by Anna Nalick*

They smile, make faces, laugh,
place trays of food on picnic tables,
carve turkeys, drop choice morsels
into the mouths of patient dogs.
                            Children
blow out birthday candles, unwrap presents.

Little boys hang from tree branches, play endless
games of catch. Little girls pour imaginary
tea into tiny cups, brush the silky
hair of dolls.
                          Women
clear the table, men lean back and smoke cigars.
There is no sound but you remember
laughter filling the air.

                        When you showed
the movies on a projector, you could rewind the film –
presents would wrap themselves up, candles would light
again, softballs would travel back
into the pitchers' hands.
                              It was like magic and always
made the kids laugh.
                                      There is no way to rewind the
years and make it all happen again. No way to
recapture the youthful face, the
slender body, the graceful fluid way of moving
you had back then.

No way to feel again
your children's soft embraces, hear their
clear bright voices. No way
to take back thoughtless words and speak
the words of love you felt but did not say.

But now there is a new bunch
of children to embrace – a chance to
get it right this time.
Maybe there is a
rewind after all.

© Mary Jones, 12/14/13

How I Want to Die

Slumped over in my armchair,
open book in my lap,
empty wine glass on the table,
a few drops of Pinot Noir left in it.
I would die in the library of my villa
in the south of France that I bought with
my lottery winnings.
My faithful maid would find me
and weep because she loved me so.
To her I was a crusty old crone
with a heart of gold
and a terrible American accent.

Or maybe I would be hit by a bus
shortly after leaving a restaurant
where I discussed my newest book with my agent.
It would be on Fifth Avenue in New York,
where I bought an apartment
after my debut novel became a best-seller.
The reading public would be devastated
and thousands would attend
my memorial service.

Or maybe I would be sitting on the beach
in Puerto Vallarta
sipping a margarita and enjoying
a mariachi band when
a rogue wave came in and swept me
into the water. Onlookers would try to save
me but to no avail.
And the band members, friends of mine,
would be grief-stricken.

I don't think I'd have a choice,
but I can dream, can't I?

© *Mary Jones, March 2017*

Late Bloomer

Seven fat buds on my
geranium plant are
hoping to bloom before the frost
kills them.
They lift their pink sweetness
to the sun in supplication.

Please
give us a chance to bloom,
We know it's late in the year
but we want to share our beauty
with the world.

I know how they feel. My days
are numbered too.

So many places I haven't traveled
So many books I've yet to read
So many songs I need to sing
So many poems inside me
          waiting to be written.

I want a chance to bloom
before the frost.

© Mary Jones, November 2015

Silence

Since he died, she can't abide the
silence of the empty house. She fills it up
with noise, talking heads on CNN,
dancing celebs on ABC, genteel
aristocrats on PBS. She turns the
stereo on full blast – Bach, Beethoven,
Brahms.

                  She doesn't
understand this since he never talked
much and the house was silent
even when he was alive. She finds it hard to eat
her solitary dinner at the kitchen table with
his empty placemat staring at her,
accusing her of what? She never cooks
anymore. What's the point of
cooking just for one?

                  And so
she gobbles down frozen dinners
in front of the TV, in front of
the latest breaking news, wars,
shootings, bombings, tornados.
Victims and survivors talk about
how it feels to go on in the face of
such tragedy, how they will pick up
the pieces of their lives.

                  She too has been
through the war, is both victim
and survivor. But no one asks how
she will cope. There is no drama here,
just the silence,
the silence and the empty house.

© *Mary Jones*

Sometimes

Sometimes she eats
chocolate cake for breakfast,
stays in her bathrobe till noon.
Sometimes she goes
to early matinees – five bucks
for seniors on Tuesdays –
and devours tubs of popcorn
drenched in fake butter.
Sometimes, after the evening news
on TV, she reads in bed
late into the night.

But sometimes she thinks
it would be nice
if he were still around
to complain
that chocolate cake isn't a
proper breakfast,
the movie was boring,
the popcorn was stale,
and her reading light
was keeping him awake.

© Mary Jones, September 2015

The Story of My Life

If I told you the story of my life, you'd
be so bored.
You'd smile and nod to be polite, but inside
you'd be wishing you were
somewhere else, like in the dentist's chair
or stuck in traffic.
Or maybe you'd suddenly
remember a previous engagement and
hastily say goodbye.
Or maybe you'd nod off, fall to the floor,
hit your head on the concrete and
suffer a concussion.
Or even die.
At your funeral, I'd sit in the back row
wearing dark glasses.
People would whisper and point.
On your tombstone, it would say
"Bored to death."

© *Mary Jones*

Walking Cliché

Mildred is not all that fond of October.
It's too damn short; besides it's cruel.
Lush gold gives way
to somber brown overnight.
It reminds her too much of her life. She used to wear

four inch heels and dance 'til dawn. Now
she wears sensible shoes and falls asleep
in her chair at nine o'clock.
She shuffles through the sodden piles of leaves and
thinks dark thoughts. Regrets
swirl 'round her feet, snap at her aching knees.

Either her ship never came in or else she
missed the boat.
She's never had a soul-mate, never
found her calling. There were
never enough hours in the day.
No time to follow her bliss.
So much water over the dam.

Now, in the twilight of her years,
what she is stuck with
is this weather-beaten body and this fading mind and
lots of memories.
She's outlived so many lovely dogs and loyal friends.
Her children all have busy lives; they
never call.

So on she walks this blustery day, each thought
darker than the one before, each cloud
heavy with shattered hopes.
She plunks her weary body on a bench
next to the pond,
black water shot through with silver stripes
by a fleeting ray of sun,
where scarlet leaves drift by like tiny sailboats.
Then something inside her smiles and her load is
lifted for awhile.

Maybe she'll go home and make an apple pie
for her husband,
who is not her soul-mate
(though she loves him anyway).
Maybe even ice cream on the top.

© *Mary Jones*

When Death Came

When the family gathered at her bedside,
they reminisced about her life,
discussed politics and weather and sports
and children and recipes.
But she was beyond caring.

When they left, taking with them
their noisy talk, leaving behind their empty
Starbucks cups and candy wrappers and
donut crumbs, she saw the events of her life
unfold before her, as though
she were a little girl again watching
autumn leaves float down
the stream behind her childhood home.
Voices and scenes from long ago, her first bike,
her first kiss, her first baby,
everything suffused with rosy light.

When Death came, it came not as a
Grim Reaper, or an Angel of Light,
but as a Compassionate Friend.
She welcomed it for she was tired
and had been ill so long.

When Death came, it came as serenely
as a winter sunrise over a frozen lake,
orange and purple and pink streaking the sky,
snow heaped high on pine branches.

When her daughter, awakened early by the
phone call, ventured out to see that sunrise,
a cardinal sang to her from the ash tree,
then flew away.

© *Mary Jones*

ACKNOWLEDGEMENTS

When Mom died in August 2021, I was devastated. Stunned, shocked, sad, surprised. What had just happened? She had just been swimming, writing and walking with friends. She had dogs to take care of and poetry to write and so so many books yet to read.

After she was gone, I spent the next six months going through everything in her 3-bedroom townhouse. It was still full of Dad's documents and books, Mom's books and records and notebooks, and 78 years of memories. There were family photos from over 150 years ago, handwritten journals from her father and stacks of her own writing.

Amongst the piles of treasures and junk, I found a three-ring binder with a sheet of paper slipped into the cover that read, "Pieces of My Mind on Paper." The binder contained print outs of the work in this book. Many of the poems had been submitted to journals, a handful had been published. Reading through them, I knew they had to be shared.

Through the encouragement and incredible support from my writing group, Patsy Kahmann, Rachel Guvenc, Marsha Partington, and Tami Mohamed Brown, this book has made it into your hands. They listened, they read, they believed. Thank you.

A special thank you to the wonderful online community at A Writing Room. They provided a safe space to write and the support of incredible writers, whom I now call friends. And a big thank you to Kim May, an incredible proofreader and friend.

To my sister, Julie Jones Stewart, thank you for being by my side since the moment we were conceived. Mom didn't necessarily want twins, but knew there was a reason she was chosen to raise us. I am grateful for you every day.

To my husband and daughter, thank you for putting up with long hours of me hiding behind a screen and for your patience and support after Mom passed. I know you both loved her and miss her.

xoxo

Jenn, Mary, and Julie, 1993

ABOUT THE AUTHORS

Mary Jensen Jones was a beloved wife, mother, sister and aunt. It is my belief that her most important role was that of grandmother to her seven grandchildren and four granddogs.

She was a writer and poet and enjoyed multiple book clubs and poetry groups. She was passionate about animals, particularly dogs. Mary was quick to open her heart and her home to others, whether it be her family and friends, her children's friends, or the many dogs she babysat at Aunt Mary's Dog Hotel. Everyone always felt welcomed by her smile, her laughter, her warmth, and her stories. Mary was an active member of Oak Grove Presbyterian Church in Bloomington, Minnesota

Jenn Jones Nienaber is a graphic designer and writer. She inherited her mother's love of dogs and words and life. She holds an MFA in creative writing from Hamline University.

She lives near Minneapolis, Minnesota with her husband, daughter and two dogs.